©2022 ALTA H MABIN
ISBN: 979-8433441842

©2024 ALTA H HAFFNER
ISBN: 978-0-7961-7664-6
ALL RIGHTS RESERVED

About the book

Writing about my dad has never been simple for me. However, I am ready to share my heartfelt feelings about this man whose words continue to resonate within me, "Keep on keeping on" - Franz P Retief.

About the author

Alta H. Haffner is a Haiku poet whose work captures the essence of precious, fleeting moments with simplicity and depth. Born with a deep appreciation for the beauty of brevity, Alta's Haiku poems reflect her keen observation of nature and her ability to evoke emotions in just a few short lines.

Drawing her inspiration from the ever-changing seasons, the delicate balance of the natural world, and the quiet whispers of every new dawn, Alta's Haiku poems invite readers to slow down, pause, and appreciate the present moment. With a handful of syllables, she allows her readers to contemplate.

Through her Haiku poetry, Alta H. Haffner reminds us of the beauty that can be found in simplicity, the power of mindfulness, and the importance of being fully present in each moment.

ALTA H HAFFNER
PUBLISHER/POET/HAIKUIST

alta@sakurabookpublishing.com
www.sakurabookpublishing.com

FOREWORD
By Charles R Haffner

Like an Eagle. A book of poems about one woman's experience with the grief of losing her father. Unfortunately, I too have experienced this pain. Regardless if it was eighteen days or eighteen years the pain is still trapped inside of us.

Alta tells her tale of this time in pieces of micropoetry. Each poem cuts a piece of her heart off and places it on the paper for us. Each memory a tear shed a smile unveiled, A moment we would trade our weight in gold to have again. Pictures of her daddy's nickname in the pages remind her of her love for him. I know for eighteen years each eagle's cry either brought a warm fuzzy feeling or a single tear. Love sometimes is funny,

What we will do to show it. Some will build a mausoleum while Alta does what writers do, She placed her heart between two covers and hopes others can understand this loss without losing the ability to smile again. May his soul fly with eagles eternally. May you read this book taking the time to pause and enjoy life.

It saddens me to realize that I will never see you again, hear your voice, but I am certain that you loved me, your little girl.

In the distant sky
a single eagle flies
watching his children
with such a deep pride
and gives his last smile

Charles R Haffner

keep on keeping on
your voice still echos daily
never forget you

Daddy, I miss you dearly
but you live inside my soul

In memory of an extraordinary man,
my daddy.

*missing
you are part of
a daily reminder
that your memory lives on now
inside*

feathers spread widely
not flying
soaring in heaven

three souls left behind
I collect feathers often
always have you close

hardly ever frowned
when you knew the end was near
you still made us laugh

I smile at a memory
your laughter was contagious

almost nineteen years
nearing the day you left us
only to live on

loved sugar popcorn
salt was forbidden to you
bribing grandsons oft'

racing
while you still told
me to please drive slowly
I ignored your voice quietly
worried

anger raged within
the day you were diagnosed
the journey begun

resting
below the bridge
flow of river water
till the end of time your soul rests
peaceful

crying at the end
you were so brave for so long
memories flowing

*your final day here
at your cold bedside we were
desperately lost*

overcome with grief
had to be strong for my boys
I just grieved alone

I took a quick call
felt like only a minute
your last breath taken

Cherish them while they're here,
And find solace in knowing
That healing will come sooner than you think.

the ocean called you
often saw dolphins dancing
binoculars zoom

not a lazy man
but watching the sports channel
snoring at halftime

many adored you
you loved life
and a song often

Eagle
given nickname
for you did know your strength
greatly admired, you were such a
rare soul

our final goodbye
chemicals kept me calmer
I collapsed with grief

*goodbyes are so hard
the long healing more painful
necessary tears*

no pretty gravesite
I scattered your ashes
alone and weeping

(I SCATTERED MY DADS ASHES AT AN EAGLE SANCTUARY)

had to let you go
holding on to your ashes
was not easy too

*painful
hiking up to
eagles nest in the heat
I wanted to do it for you
felt good*

waterfall beneath
two eggs of baby eagles
only one will live

The sad reality is that only a single chick will grow to adulthood. The reason for this being a phenomena called Cainism (or in other words a Cain and Abel struggle) whereby the stronger of the two chicks (usually the oldest (Cain), attacks and eventually kills and devours its sibling (Abel) after a 3 to 4 day struggle.

the most beautiful
mix of aloe and roses
crying at the bridge

final call to me
oh, you knew the end was near
final I love you

it was not easy
knowing your voice will fade soon
heaven calling you

rainbows
brightest colors
not seen for a while now
only thunderous storms and rain
crying

eagle
my daddy strong
to the world outside him
helping others grow more than him
hero

dark grey skies above
hurting deep
will I find peace soon

pensive thoughts today
write about your memory
so much I blocked out

*you called me little
even though I grew up quick
always be your kid*

motivation spoke
when you entered a full room
all mattered to you

*I remembered when
you made them listen, hear you
a soft voice within*

she gave her whole half
it was good enough, daddy
purest gift to us

climbing many stairs
tired, desperately trying
to get to you fast

was often too late for lunch
your bland dinner was cold too

forgetting your voice
the voicemail reminders now
the dreaded redials

*I celebrate you
daily by following my
biggest dreams and goals*

last forehead kisses
believed you could still hear me
say I love you dad

missing
you are harder
when all I don't hear now
is your voice of wisdom and hope
a void

fighting back the tears
I write to your memory
more pain than joy now

conflict
is there a God
I simply just wanted
you breathing here again with us
let go

family divide
years of not understanding
maybe peace will come

days and nights the same
I can't tell the difference
you are still gone, dad

was all dressed in black
pale pastel pink silky scarf
all said our goodbyes

darkest thoughts linger
alcohol consumed nightly
trying to drown pain

hues of grey and black
try to remember your face
faded to just black

today I made plans
move away from this city
brand new start for me

I feared I will forget you
but you remained in my heart

contemplating days
so far from your resting place
hope to visit soon

with your final call
you witnessed pure white roses
never to see one

light summer rainfall
tears I cried
while trying to smile

fall into slumber
all my nightly prayers vanished
without you breathing

*she felt so much pain
empty bottles her solace
waiting patiently*

weeks after you died
a small pink chapel wedding
he broke my soul deep

seaside holidays
children swimming and laughing
the joy you gave us

grief of losing you
my pain trapped inside my heart
even eagles cry

*Emoyeni was born
two years after you left us
nature gave me hope*

sound of an eagle
sun over heavens blue rays
between the white clouds

*you are free of pain
the pain lives inside me now
and forevermore*

*the morning whispers
birds but not a great eagle
gone out of sight now*

eagle flying high
beyond the rocky mountains
sacred memories

miss you every day
feelings I let go slowly
we meet again soon

soft autumn colors
sun peeping at my window
soon I will let go

for now, let me remember
in my heart little longer

rose petals falling
piano music playing
final words of love

thank you daddy, I love you
always and forevermore

The eagle
simply represents
the man I use to
call Daddy...
and always will.

For me, I know my daddy is with me every day, every waking moment.

They say it is the hardest to lose your first parent, I do agree but then how do you cope knowing the pain you endured?

How will you begin to understand that it will never be the same again?
How do you come to terms with knowing that dreaded call could come when you are least ready?

Thank you for taking the time to read my gift to the memory of my daddy, a man that will be remembered always, with both tears and laughter.

~ Alta H Haffner

More books by Alta H Haffner

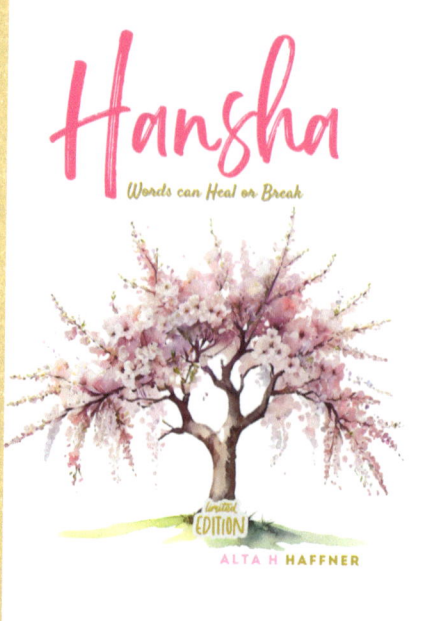

www.ingramcontent.com/pod-product-compliance
Lightning Source LLC
Chambersburg PA
CBHW042044290426
44109CB00001B/22